by Tatenda Shamiso

॥SAMUEL FRENCH॥

FOR AMATEUR PRODUCTION ENQUIRIES

UNITED KINGDOM AND WORLD
EXCLUDING NORTH AMERICA
licensing@concordtheatricals.co.uk

020-7054-7298

Each title is subject to availability from Concord Theatricals, depending upon country of performance.

NO I.D. was first performed at Theatre Peckham on Wednesday 4 May 2022, and at the Royal Court Jerwood Theatre Upstairs, London, on Tuesday 18 April 2023. The cast was as follows:

TATENDA . . . . Tatenda Shamiso

VOICE CREDITS:
ANDREW . . . . Rufus Love
AUTOMATED PHONE VOICE . . . . Lauren Semme

OTHER VOICES:
Aaron Beaudin, Delaney Bird, Claudia Casino, Esther Ngonidzashe Chimanga, Hannah Cole, Julianne Downing, Rodion Galiullin, Connor Heaney, Dafne Louzioti, Lora Nikolova, Lewis Pickles, Lauren Tranter, Jay Lafayette Valentine, Sean Ting-Hsuan Wang, Hans Van Wesenbeeck, Naomi Van Wesenbeeck & Thandiwe

CREATIVE TEAM
Writer & Performer | Tatenda Shamiso
Director | Sean Ting-Hsuan Wang
Designer | Claudia Casino
Original Lighting Designer | Zoe Beeny
Stage Manager | Ting (Yi-Ting) Huang
Producer | Dylan Marc Verley

Special thanks to Gabriel Dedji for providing musical arrangements.

CAST AND CREATIVE

TATENDA SHAMISO | WRITER & PERFORMER

Tatenda (he/him) is a theatre-maker, writer and musician with origins from Zimbabwe, Belgium, the United States and Switzerland. He is also a scholarly researcher in Afrofuturism and its potential to deconstruct and rebuild our notions of gender, space and time. Tatenda freelances as a writer, director and facilitator, and guest lectures in the Theatre and Performance Department at Goldsmiths, University of London.

As writer & performer, theatre includes: *NO I.D.* (Theatre Peckham & VAULT Festival).

As actor, theatre includes: *Sundown Kiki* (Young Vic); *Bootycandy* (Gate – cover); *drop dead gorgeous* (VAULT Festival).

As writer & director, theatre includes: *Housewarming* (Theatre Peckham).

As assistant director, theatre includes: *A Streetcar Named Desire* (Almeida & Phoenix); *Bootycandy* (Gate).

As co-writer & dramaturg, theatre includes: *The Village* (Almeida Young Company).

Awards include: VAULT Award for Show of the Week (*NO I.D.*), Nominated for Offies Award for Best Performance Piece (*NO I.D.*).

SEAN TING-HSUAN WANG | DIRECTOR

Sean (he/him) is a Taiwanese director, performer and educator. He has directed Tatenda in *NO I.D.* since its inception at Theatre Peckham. Sean's solo work centres around impulses, playing with anticipation and physical memory, all in relation to music and movement.

As director, theatre includes: *NO I.D.* (Theatre Peckham & Vault Festival).

As movement director, theatre includes: *The Frontline* (Theatre Peckham); *Sunny Side Up* (Theatre Peckham); *Dark Matter* (VAULT Festival).

As actor, theatre includes: *Human Nature* (好時光咖啡); *Housewarming* (Theatre Peckham); *Home Sweet Home* (Taipei-London, Online).

CLAUDIA CASINO | DESIGNER

Claudia (she/her) is a Spatial Designer focused on Immersive, Experience, and Performance Design. She is currently completing her MA in Narrative Environments at Central Saint Martins.

As designer, theatre includes: *NO I.D.* (Theatre Peckham & VAULT Festival); *Housewarming* (Theatre Peckham); *Madrigal* (Courtyard Theatre).

As assistant designer, theatre includes: *Indecent Proposal* (Southwark Playhouse).

ZOE BEENY | ORIGINAL LIGHTING DESIGNER

Zoe Beeny (they/she) is a Lighting Designer and Technician. After completing their degree in Drama and English at Goldsmiths, University of London, they have gone on to work as a technician at The Bridge Theatre and The National Theatre.

As lighting designer, theatre includes: *NO I.D.* (Theatre Peckham & VAULT Festival); *Housewarming* (Cockpit & Theatre Peckham); *RIP Everyone, Eventually* (Bread and Roses Theatre, Clapham Fringe Festival); *Eden* (Matchstick); *Precious Little Talent* (Courtyard).

TING (YI-TING) HUANG | STAGE MANAGER

Ting (she/her) is a London & Taiwan based stage manager, theatre-maker and artist with a passion for cross-cultural and interdisciplinary collaborations, including movement, live art, installations and contemporary art exhibitions.

As stage manager, theatre includes: *Housewarming* (Theatre Peckham); *Mundane Greenhouse* (Taipei Performing Arts Center).

As scenic artist, theatre includes: *The Forgotten, The Weight of Things, All That Remains* (Riverbed Theatre, Taiwan).

As deviser & performer, theatre includes: *drop dead gorgeous* (Edinburgh Festival Fringe, VAULT Festival, Taiwan Contemporary Cultural Lab).

Awards include: Nominated for VAULT Festival for Innovation Award & The Origins Award (*drop dead gorgeous*).

DYLAN MARC VERLEY | PRODUCER

Dylan (he/him) is a producer, director, writer and experimental creative. He is currently working in commercial theatre sector, specialising in touring theatre.

As producer, theatre includes: *NO I.D.* (VAULT Festival); *Along the Coast* (Piece of Cake Productions).

As assistant producer, theatre includes: *Sundown Kiki* (Young Vic).

As director, theatre includes: *Foxes* (Assistant Director, Seven Dials); *Foxes* (Associate Director, Brits on Broadway).

As writer, theatre includes: *Three Islands* (Talawa Young People); *Road Safety* (Barnet Council); *Ice Blunts* (Young Vic); *Order Up* (Royal Central School of Speech and Drama).

As actor, theatre includes: *The Route* (Bush); *Order Up* (Royal Central School of Speech and Drama).

Production assistant credits: *The Cher Show, The Osmonds, Johannes Radebe: Freedom, Johannes Radebe Freedom: Unleashed, Oti Mabuse: I Am Here, Fisherman's Friends: The Musical* (ROYO, UK Tour).

THE ROYAL COURT THEATRE

The Royal Court Theatre is the writers' theatre. It is a leading force in world theatre for cultivating and supporting writers – undiscovered, emerging and established.

Through the writers, the Royal Court is at the forefront of creating restless, alert, provocative theatre about now. We open our doors to the unheard voices and free thinkers that, through their writing, change our way of seeing.

Over 120,000 people visit the Royal Court in Sloane Square, London, each year and many thousands more see our work elsewhere through transfers to the West End and New York, UK and international tours, digital platforms, our residencies across London, and our site-specific work. Through all our work we strive to inspire audiences and influence future writers with radical thinking and provocative discussion.

The Royal Court's extensive development activity encompasses a diverse range of writers and artists and includes an ongoing programme of writers' attachments, readings, workshops and playwriting groups. Twenty years of the International Department's pioneering work around the world means the Royal Court has relationships with writers on every continent.

Since 1956 we have commissioned and produced hundreds of writers, from John Osborne to Jasmine Lee-Jones. Royal Court plays from every decade are now performed on stage and taught in classrooms and universities across the globe.

We strive to create an environment in which differing voices and opinions can co-exist. In current times, it is becoming increasingly difficult for writers to write what they want or need to write without fear, and we will do everything we can to rise above a narrowing of viewpoints.

It is because of this commitment to the writer and our future that we believe there is no more important theatre in the world than the Royal Court.

🐦 royalcourt f royalcourttheatre

Supported using public funding by
ARTS COUNCIL ENGLAND

ROYAL COURT SUPPORTERS

Our incredible community of supporters makes it possible for us to achieve our mission of nurturing and platforming writers at every stage of their careers. Our supporters are part of our essential fabric – they help to give us the freedom to take bigger and bolder risks in our work, develop and empower new voices, and create world-class theatre that challenges and disrupts the theatre ecology.

To all our supporters, thank you. You help us to write the future.

CHARACTERS

TATENDA
ANDREW (VOICE)
AUTOMATED PHONE VOICE

OTHER VOICES

FRIEND 1
FRIEND 2
FRIEND 3
FRIEND 4
FRIEND 5
FRIEND 6
FRIEND 7
TATENDA'S MOM
TATENDA'S DAD
THANDIE
FULLY INSANE SOUNDING DOCTOR
PSYCHIATRIST
PHONE VOICES

SETTING

Tatenda's home, which over the course of the show is invaded and overrun by paperwork, archival boxes, overflowing filing cabinets.

TIME

Early 2020

AUTHOR'S NOTE

This play is intended to celebrate and give voice to a perspective on the Global Majority trans experience. Any company intending to stage this should keep this in mind when casting – Tatenda is a person of colour unequivocally.

For the trans siblings who are too busy defending their very existence to write a little play about it.

(**TATENDA** *enters at the edge of the stage, where a clunky old school telephone sits.*)

(*Phone ringing.*)

AUTOMATED PHONE VOICE. Welcome to the NO I.D. phone line. For English, press one.

(*Beep.*)

Your call is very important to us. Please wait until you have heard all of the following options before making your selection.

If you would like to hear vague marketing information regarding tonight's performance that you can already find on the website, please press one.

If you would like to establish your identity in order to receive basic public services and exercise your human rights under Article 22 of the United Nations Declaration of 1948, please press two.

(*Beep.*)

Please wait until you have heard all of the following options before making your selection.

If you would like to hear vague marketing information regarding tonight's performance –

TATENDA. Fuck's sake.

AUTOMATED PHONE VOICE. – that you can already find on the website, please press one.

If you would like to establish your identity in order to receive basic public services and exercise your human rights under Article 22 of the United Nations Declaration of 1948, please press two.

AUTOMATED PHONE VOICE.   If you would like to experience the performance you paid to attend this evening, please press three.

>   *(Beep.)*

Sorry, all of our basic human rights advisers are busy at the moment. In the meantime the performance will begin.

You are currently user number – five – in the queue.

>   *(Waiting music.)*

>   (**TATENDA***'s head begins bopping along to the song subtly.)*

You are currently user number – four – in the queue.

>   *(Waiting music.)*

>   *(He's getting his shoulders into it now. This song is very familiar to him.)*

You are currently user number – three – in the queue.

>   *(Waiting music.)*

>   *(It's kind of his jam. He gets up to dance.)*

You are currently user number – one – in the queue.

>   *(He's fully bopping to the track. Arms. Legs. Drama.)*

>   *(Phone ringing.)*

>   (**TATENDA** *rushes back to the phone receiver.)*

ANDREW. NO I.D. phone service, my name is Andrew, how can I help you today?

TATENDA. Hi, I was wondering if I could make an amendment to my public record.

ANDREW. Could you be a bit more specific?

TATENDA. I'm trying to change my name and gender marker in all of my identity documents and public records.

ANDREW. I see… is this because you –

TATENDA. Yes, I'm transgender.

ANDREW. I see. Thank you for providing this information.

TATENDA. No worries, I had to.

ANDREW. And you are transitioning from –

TATENDA. Female to male.

ANDREW. Okay. May I take your name please?

TATENDA. Of course, it's Tatenda Shamiso.

ANDREW. Ta – ten – da? So that's T – A –

TATENDA. Tango Alpha Tango Echo November Delta Alpha. And my surname is Shamiso, Sierra Hotel Alpha Mother Indigo Sierra Oscar.

ANDREW. Thank you. And can I please take your previous name?

TATENDA. Yeah it was Thandiwe Van Wesenbeeck. You need me to spell that for you?

ANDREW. *(Embarrassed.)* Yes please.

TATENDA. That's

THANDIWE,

Tango Hotel Alpha November Delta Indigo Whiskey Echo,

VAN,

Victor Alpha November,

Space,

TATENDA. WESENBEECK,

Whiskey Echo Sierra Echo November Bravo Echo Echo Charlie Kilo.

ANDREW. T – H – A – N – D – I – W – E, V – A – N, W – E – S – E – N – V – E – E – C – K.

TATENDA. Yes, uh, that's B – E – E – C – K, right?

ANDREW. V – E – E – C – K.

TATENDA. Sorry, V for Victor or B for bravo?

ANDREW. V for Victor.

TATENDA. It's actually B for Bravo.

ANDREW. My apologies. So to recap, that's actually T – H – A – N – D – I – W – E, V – A – N, W – E – S – E – N – B – E – E – C – K

> (**TATENDA** *spells out his name with his body, cheerleader style. He gets the K wrong.*)

TATENDA. – No.

ANDREW. K.

> (**TATENDA** *gets the K the right way around.*)

TATENDA. Yes.

ANDREW. And that's the name you don't want.

TATENDA. Yes, it always surprises people why.

ANDREW. Well it's very unique.

TATENDA. Thanks.

ANDREW. May I take down your nationality?

TATENDA. Sure, I'm a dual Belgian and American citizen but I'll also need the records changed in the UK and Switzerland.

ANDREW. Belgian and American, interesting... where does your first name come from?

TATENDA. I don't see how that's relevant but it's from Zimbabwe. My mother's from there.

ANDREW. And you don't have a Zimbabwean citizenship?

TATENDA. No.

ANDREW. Saves on paper I suppose.

(Awkward pause.)

Well Miss – my apologies, do you prefer to go by Miss or Mister? Or is it Mx?

TATENDA. Mister.

ANDREW. Right, well Mr. Shamiso, unfortunately I'm sure you're aware that the NO I.D. phone line doesn't actually exist, and you'll need to sort this out on your own.

TATENDA. Yes.

ANDREW. Is there another reason you phoned us today?

TATENDA. Nah. I was just sort of hoping I could explain everything once, so I don't have to explain it again.

ANDREW. Well, thank you very much for calling.

TATENDA. Uh, thank you.

ANDREW. Is there anything else I can help you with today?

TATENDA. I do need to rehearse my next phone call to HMRC?

ANDREW. Alright, go ahead.

THE PROBLEM

TATENDA. Last year I registered a business to make my art under my name. My actual name, not my old one. It was pretty easy. I registered with the Companies House and opened a business bank account without having to show a single form of identification.

Since then I've moved house twice, and I haven't filed my taxes once. And all of my business's mail gets sent to my old address. And I'm too scared to call them.

I don't know what will happen if I do. I'm pretty sure it'll be straightforward, but I can't shake the feeling that they're going to ask the kinds of questions that make it look as if I'm committing fraud.

I'm too scared to call a lot of numbers. HMRC, the Student Loans Company, the Belgian Embassy, a solicitor, the GP, the Foreign, Commonwealth & Development Office, the surgeon who I'd like to remove my breasts...

I think the smallest fish right now is Her Majesty's – oh, sorry – **His,** Majesty's Revenue and Customs.

(Easy for some.)

But if they ask why I've got a National Insurance number under someone else's name, I need to have a clear and concise answer.

All I have to do is prove that Thandie and I are the same person.

I should probably start with her.

THANDIWE

(While **TATENDA** *enters further into the space, revealing his room, which is littered with loose papers, recordings of his friends and loved ones play. He tidies the space while his loved ones explain what kind of girl* **THANDIE** *was.)*

FRIEND 1. Thandie was a gem. She always lit up the room wherever she went.

FRIEND 2. Thandie was the kind of girl who would make you feel welcome.

FRIEND 3. I first met Thandie when we were fourteen and my first impression of her was, "oh my god, she's *so cool*" –

FRIEND 4. – Everyone wanted to be friends with her and talk to her all the time.

FRIEND 5. Thandie was the person who I could tell my secrets to, and I was the person that had Thandie's secrets.

FRIEND 6. When we would hang out between the ages of five through nine, Thandie would take off her shirt, and just, you know, live life. So free.

FRIEND 5. Thandie was more focused on Kristen Stewart when the rest of us were fighting over Edward versus Jacob.

FRIEND 2. We were like the two little emo shits in the group.

FRIEND 7. – Always put together, but if you pointed it out, she'd insist she was really a mess.

FRIEND 1. She always was very energetic and made everybody feel like they were valid, just like, no matter how stupid or weird they were acting.

FRIEND 6. When we were between the ages of like five and six, I forced Thandie to do a summer camp with me, and it was a theatre camp. And that was Thandie's worst nightmare. She literally begged her mom, "Please don't make me do this camp with Hannah. That's. The last thing I would ever want to do with my free time." And uh, she very soon became the star of the camp. And to this day I really love to take credit for that.

FRIEND 5. Thandie played Annie way before it was cool for little black girls to play Annie.

FRIEND 3. I believe she was a people-pleaser. She had a hard time saying no to people.

FRIEND 4. Being her close friend, I saw that the attention stressed her out so much. I think it was because everyone always wanted something from her? It was kind of weird, she wasn't some spectacle, she was just a normal girl –

FRIEND 3. She just wanted to see others happy –

FRIEND 1. – Brought a lot of passion to pretty much anything that she set her mind to –

FRIEND 3. – And she wasn't afraid to call people out when she needed to.

TATENDA'S MOM. Thandie was the sweetest and most precocious little girl. She would surprise us with her knowledge of the most random things. When she was four, she decided to get into the habit of stealing books... we used to meet friends at a bookstore called Cody's, on Fourth Street in Berkeley, every Friday. And for some reason Thandie decided it was a good idea to steal books rather than ask me if she could have them. It was very random things that she... just, so precocious. And hilarious, actually, because it was always like, this great kid, and then she'd be just, shocking me with the most... random, random things. Just a really all-round fun and surprising character. And you'd think as a mother that I would know my kid but she... has never stopped surprising me!

(She laughs.)

But thank God for that, right?

(Beat.)

TATENDA. I was born a girl. Please try to contain your surprise.

I was born an American girl, in California, to a Zimbabwean mother and a Belgian father.

I was the girl with the big hair, with the even bigger voice, the girl who always brought snacks, the girl who would do your homework for you if you were pretty...

Not gonna lie, Thandie knew everyone. She wasn't particularly popular with people her age, she was a little bit too openly nerdy to pass as cool, she was honestly kind of a lot, but everybody knew her.

Thandie was a musical theatre kid, for better or worse. It protected her from the potential severity of the racial bullying at her school, because she was visible. Always onstage. You'd notice if someone fucked with her.

It did still subject her to the standard bullying you'd get for being a musical theatre kid. But that builds character.

She did Model United Nations, too. She was an advocate. She would get asked to give speeches about how Super-Inclusive-And-Not-Homophobic her school was when important people came to visit. Always the first to raise her hand in debate class. It was so hard to keep up with her. She danced, she wrote, she obsessed over *Harry Potter* – she fucking loved *Harry Potter*. She put JK Rowling right up there next to Jesus.

She was an incredibly sweet young girl. It was so hard to keep up with her.

*(A video plays: we see **THANDIE** performing in* Anything Goes, *senior year of high school. It's the tap dance section of the titular song.* **TATENDA** *lip-syncs and dances along to mixed success and eventually completely fails at the end of the big tap section.)*

(Lightly panting.) It's so hard to keep up with her.

TATENDA. Thandiwe means 'she who is loved'. I think it really suited me.

(Beat.)

(Gesturing towards his body.) I'll show you this now so you don't have to be curious for the rest of this.

*(**TATENDA** begins to undress, down to a bralette and briefs. He's not thrilled about it.)*

And there you have it. A trans body, ta-da.

*(Throughout this section **TATENDA** tries on a variety of ladies clothes.)*

Now, I don't know how familiar anyone in the audience is with being assigned female at birth, but I at least found you get taught that being a girl comes with discomfort.

(He retrieves an office-style archive box from the edge of the stage, opens it, and pulls out a little black dress. He begins to pull it on.)

It starts with very simple stuff. You're going to have to wait and wait for a wonderful man to sweep you off your feet and give you a happy life, like in Disney movies.

(To a member of the audience, coyly.) I'm sorry, you're so handsome – could you zip me up?

> *(He enters the audience to receive help zipping. Once zipped he returns to the stage.)*

You're going to wear makeup and pretty high heels, but not too early. You have to wait to become beautiful.

> *(He starts trying to unzip the dress, reaching behind his back, but can't quite manage it.)*

You're going to go to school and boys will be mean to you when they like you. It's important to tolerate this kind of abuse if you're to find a prince charming.

> *(He runs to the same member of the audience, asking them to help unzip the dress.)*

Thanks so much.

> *(He returns to the office box and pulls out another little outfit, gets dressed again.)*

You're going to meet other girls; some who are nice, and some who are mean. You're going to be mean to the mean girls with the girls who are nice. You're going to learn how to navigate 'drama'.

You will not be taken seriously when your feelings are hurt. You are taught that girls cry. It's in their nature. They just cry. You're probably not hurt, really. You're probably just a girl. Silly girl.

You're going to bleed. You're going to ache. And you cannot tell anyone about it. You will not find a prince charming –

> *(He gives a flirty wave to his dressing assistant in the audience.)*

(Whispering.) – if he knows that you bleed.

(Back to the box, undress, next outfit.)

TATENDA. You're going to learn that sometimes, in the interest of community, you will need to pretend like you are madly in love with Harry Styles, or Justin Bieber, or Taylor Lautner. You will learn to channel your envy of these young men into crushes, probably without realizing.

You will learn to turn your real crushes into something quiet and small, probably without realising.

When you can finally wear the makeup and the heels and the skirts and the blouses you might find they aren't as comfortable as you expected. But you will learn to carry yourself in these things with pride because beauty is pain, darling.

You're going to need to give your body to whoever asks for it, but with great tact. You'll be a prude no matter what you do, and you'll be a slut no matter what you don't do.

Oh, and you're going to have to smell nice, always.

Don't get me wrong, being a girl was wonderful in so many ways. The friendships are deeper. The **bathrooms**. Are **nicer**. But learning these things, I figured that being a girl was just uncomfortable by nature. I thought I would grow into it. I waited a long time to grow into it.

It's not the first growth spurt I skipped.

It wasn't just hard to keep up with Thandie. I think it was hard for her to keep up with herself. I think she moved fast, threw herself into something, and the next thing, and the next thing, cause if she stopped, she'd notice how... heavy. She felt. If she ever lost momentum.

She wrote music about that sometimes –

(A recording plays: **THANDIE** *singing a song she wrote called "girl".* **TATENDA** *plays along with whatever instrument he feels like playing that night, either the guitar or keyboard. He might sing along if he feels like it.)*

THANDIE.
I CARRY MORE THAN JUST MYSELF
I HOIST, I HEAVE
MY SOUL SOARS PAST THIS PLANET
MY BODY WEIGHS ME DOWN
I BLEED IT'S NO BIG DEAL
I PATCH IT UP BUT IT WON'T HEAL
I BLEED IT'S NO BIG DEAL
I PATCH IT UP BUT IT WON'T HEAL
I WANNA HOLD YOU LIKE I'M SEVEN FEET TALL
I CURL UP INTO A LITTLE BALL
WANNA LIFT UP MY FAMILY, THE WAY A GOOD MAN
    SHOULD
BUT I WISH ANYBODY ELSE COULD
I BLEED IT'S NO BIG DEAL
I PATCH IT UP BUT IT WON'T HEAL
I BLEED IT'S NO BIG DEAL
I PATCH IT UP BUT IT WON'T HEAL

*(***THANDIE***'s voice continues in the background.)*

TATENDA. I'm sure there's a scientific principle that explains how everything at some point loses momentum. Everything that starts moving, stops moving, at some point, right? Or maybe they go on forever? I think she thought she'd go on like that forever. But then she got into art school – I got into art school.

TATENDA. We both did.

*(***TATENDA***, having quite a visceral, uncomfortable time having sat in the girly*

outfit for this long, rushes towards another archive box. He pulls out a binder, a pair of trousers and a plain t-shirt. He changes clothes as quickly as possible, relaxing as each piece of feminine clothing is replaced with its masculine counterpart.)

(As he dresses, the song finishes.)

THANDIE.
BLEED
NO BIG DEAL
PATCH IT UP BUT
IT WON'T HEAL

BLEED
NO BIG DEAL
PATCH IT UP BUT
IT DON'T HEAL, NO

BLEED
NO BIG DEAL
PATCH IT UP BUT
IT DON'T HEAL, NO

BLEED
NO BIG DEAL
PATCH IT UP
IT DON'T HEAL

SOMETIMES BEFRIENDING TRANNIES MAKES IT HARD TO STAY CIS

TATENDA. Don't tell anyone I said this, but thank god for Goldsmiths.

I discovered I wasn't a girl when I was nineteen.

I don't know how it happened, really. I didn't have any sort of magical come-to-tranny-Jesus moment where everything clicked. It was just time. I had queer friends. I had a septum piercing. I was studying avant-garde theatre. I had recently contracted and recovered from a cute and casual STI. Everyone around me understood that gender is a construct and that *everyday life is a performance* ---- you know what I mean?

That year I was in a dance piece about performing femininity. Thandie loved shit like that. I'm a feminist thanks to her.

One day after a rehearsal, I started to notice...

Even when we finished in the studio, my performance of femininity never really ended. I was always on the clock, putting it on, on the street, in the bus, back at home.

By this point, in my mind, I had mastered the art of being a girl. I think that was the issue. I was doing everything right and I was still waiting for it to feel okay. And it just didn't. So I started to wonder if I was ever meant to grow in that direction.

I had no idea what I was doing, so I read a lot of Judith Butler, and it didn't make any sense, but I felt more justified in the feelings bubbling up to my surface. Thandie wasn't an angry person, ever, but I – she – ? – was getting angry. I was so angry at the systems I had taken as gospel from my birth. Countless systems based on the arbitrary decisions of a handful of colonists.

TATENDA. I spent the following few months alone in my room with my antiracist queer theory, digesting the reality of our situation here. Learning about the alternatives. I'll walk you through it really quickly.

> (**TATENDA** *pulls out two stacks of the same archive boxes with male and female restroom signs on them.*)

Right.

Gender in Europe looks like this.

> (*He opens one of the boxes on the male sign to reveal a massive dildo, lit up from inside the box.*)

And a lot of the rest of the world now, too. But it didn't always!

> (*He begins to distort the signs throughout the next section, placing different sections of the bathroom signs in different piles, remixing the images.*)

Indigenous cultures all over the world both had and have insanely diverse gender categories, many which aren't at all tied to anatomy, and they're generally much more flexible than the binary European system. And, here's a kicker, people could often move between them and beyond them. And they still fucking can. Are you keeping up with me? Is it hard to keep up with me?

I want to get more specific, but you get the point. Anyways it's hard to pin down the details. A lot of it got lost as a result of colonialism. But I know I felt it as soon as I read these things – my ancestors probably don't give a fuck what it says on my birth certificate.

I started thinking of my gender expression like designing a Sim, or dressing a Barbie doll. Endless possibilities and presentations.

There is so much space between feminine and masculine. An uninterrupted breeze. Fresh, fresh air.
I learned to make room for parts of myself that I used to instinctively silence. I learned to let go of things that confined me.

I found that my spirit could let go of colonial femininity with ease, but my reflection served as a daily reminder of the way everyone else still saw me. No matter how they/them I was dressed that day.

Once again I thought I had solved the problem, but I didn't know how to explain why I felt that my hips don't speak for me. My tits gave me away as a person in discomfort. My voice, beautiful as it was, didn't sound like a voice that belonged to the person I was becoming. I felt shifty under my skin. And as much as I can't stand the binary, I kept feeling myself shifting further and further towards the masculine side of the line. All I knew for sure was that my gender dysphoria was making it harder to get through the day.

And then I found out that I could get help with this for free under the NHS?!
And then I found out that it would take me at least four years to get to the top of their waiting lists.
And then I got angry.
And then I found out that private clinics can see you in a matter of weeks!
And then I found out how much it would cost to get to a private clinic.
And then I got angry.
And then I spent a lot of time angry, and defeated.
A lot of time.

Thandie did not know how to ask for help. She always preferred to keep who she was and what she needed hidden from herself, let alone anyone else. So I am so grateful to the beautiful people who saw her finally ask, and answered.

TATENDA. Thandiwe, again, means 'she who is loved'. Tatenda means 'thank you'.

I wanted to thank them for the love that made Thandie who she was. And thank them for the space to become the person I am.

    (**TATENDA** *picks up the phone.*)

    (*Phone ringing.*)

AUTOMATED PHONE VOICE. Welcome to the London Transgender Clinic. For the hormone clinic, press one.

    (*Beep.*)

We're sorry, all of our agents are busy at the moment. This telephone queue will charge twenty pounds per second...

    (*Waiting music, for just a second.*)

    (**TATENDA** *hangs up.*)

TATENDA. Anyone who wants to medically transition in the United Kingdom has to supply a clinical diagnosis of gender dysphoria from a licensed psychiatrist.

It's a little bit like standing trial. You are cisgender until proven quirky. I had heard from some of my friends that the questions my psychiatrist would ask might at times feel a bit black-or-white, and that it might feel wrong, but at the end of the day you sometimes also need to **perform** transness. To get the ticks in the boxes you need, you must tell your story with no gray area.

Five hundred donated pounds later, I was sat in front of a psychiatrist approved by the London Transgender Clinic.

FULLY INSANE SOUNDING DOCTOR. DID YOU PLAY WITH LEGOS, OR BARBIES, AS A CHILD?

TATENDA. Uh, Legos.

FULLY INSANE SOUNDING DOCTOR. DID YOU HAVE MORE MALE OR FEMALE FRIENDS IN SCHOOL?

TATENDA. Male.

FULLY INSANE SOUNDING DOCTOR. DID YOU PREFER. BLUE. OR PINK.

TATENDA. Blue.

My diagnosis:

> *(An image is projected displaying the text:*
> ***Gender dysphoria (ICD-10 F64.0, DSM-5***
> ***302.85).)***

In one hour –

> *(He reveals a cascading roll of paperwork*
> *that extends past the length of the stage.)*

– the doctor railed through my gender identity history, a summary of my transition, my past psychiatric history, my family history, my personal history, my psychosexual history, collateral history *(collected from my flatmate)*, a mental state examination, a mental capacity assessment, and finished with his opinion and recommendation. I didn't get out of bed for two days afterwards. He wrung me dry. But I got what I needed.

> *(A recording of the* **PSYCHIATRIC** *report*
> *plays. Let the reader be informed that this*
> *is a heavily abridged version of the original*
> *report; you're welcome xoxo.)*

PSYCHIATRIST. Mr Shamiso reports a history of gender dysphoria dating back to his childhood. At the age of seven he realised that he felt different to other girls and that he did not fit in with them. He enjoyed wearing boys' clothing, including his school uniform, and felt particular pleasure when mistaken for a boy by members of the public.

At first, he thought that perhaps he would grow into accepting his assigned female gender. Instead, he began to feel 'disgusted' when his body started changing during puberty, growing breasts and beginning to menstruate. The idea that he one day might become pregnant seemed 'revolting' to him.

Mr Shamiso is currently suffering from dysphoria about his breasts, his high-pitched speaking voice, his lack of facial and body hair and his feminine body shape. It affects his mood and triggers anxiety. He feels disconnected from his body and describes the feeling of seeing one's body in a different way to everyone else as 'isolating'. He finds being misgendered by others upsetting. His sense of dysphoria is also impacting his academic performance at university.

I obtained collateral history from his flatmate, who confirmed that she has known Mr Shamiso for the past two years, always as a man. She reports that in the time she has known him, she has seen his psychological state deteriorate as his sense of gender dysphoria intensified. She has no concerns about his gender permanence.

On mental state examination today, Mr Shamiso presented as a well kempt, appropriately dressed transgender man with short hair. He established appropriate, polite rapport and good eye contact. There was no psychomotor disturbance on examination. His speech was normal in volume, rate and tone, and he was articulate in outlining his difficulties. He reported having good energy levels, adequate sleep, a normal appetite and libido. He denied any suicidal ideation or plans and denied having any aggressive thoughts. I did not observe or elicit any psychotic phenomena or perceptual abnormalities.

He scored twenty on Core-10, eighteen on PHQ-9 and eighteen on GAD-7, indicating moderately severe psychological distress, moderately severe depression and severe anxiety, in line with his psychiatric history and my clinical observations, and which are most likely arising from his gender dysphoria.

He is aware that Testosterone therapy is likely to affect the pitch of his voice, on which he relies for his artistic expression, but he is prepared to accept the risk that it may become less appealing to others.

My overall initial impression is that Mr Shamiso has been suffering from gender dysphoria since his early childhood. The symptoms he reports, as outlined in his gender history section of this report, have lasted well over six months and satisfy the diagnostic criteria for gender dysphoria (DSM-5, 302.85); this has resulted in significant psychological distress and functional impairment.

TATENDA. I got what I needed. I was impaired, distressed, disgusted, but I got what I needed.

> *(He sits.)*

I'd like you to know that when I was four, I had a Princess Belle dress, and I loved it more than anything else I owned.
Halloween 2007, I went as a diva.
I loved Barbies.
I hated Lego.

TATENDA. I was OBSESSED with boys.
My doctor couldn't know that, but you can.

> *(A song plays: hard to say if it was written by **THANDIE** or **TATENDA**. It is called "skin." **TATENDA** sings and plays along with this recording, improvising vocals above the*

*refrain of the track, which loops until he's
exhausted himself a little.)*

THANDIE/TATENDA.

MY RAGE
TURNS MY TONGUE TO FLAMES
YOU'RE NOT TO BLAME
WHY I CAN'T BE TAMED, NO,
DON'T TAME ME,

EBBS AND FLOWS
PUSH ME DOWN A SLOPE
YOU'RE NOT TO BLAME, NO
YOU DON'T HAVE TO SAY SO
JUST DON'T LET ME GO
I JUST

STILL CAN'T STAND IT
IN MY SKIN I
STILL DON'T LIKE THE
STATE I'M IN I
STILL CAN'T STAND IT
IN MY SKIN I
STILL DON'T LIKE THE
STATE I'M IN

HE/HIM

TATENDA. On December third, 2020, I supplied the London Transgender Clinic with a registration form, my passport (in the wrong name), an unenrolled deed poll, a medical questionnaire, a shared care request with my GP, my psychiatric report, some blood, some piss, and a stupid amount of money. In return they gave me some pokes, some prods, and my first prescription of Testogel.

They asked me in my appointment why I hadn't changed my name yet. I told them I just hadn't gotten around to it. Between my EU Settlement Scheme status, National Insurance, my NHS number, bank accounts, two passports, I was worried it would be a hassle. Figured I'd wait.

> *(Pause.)*

Andrew?

Andrew? From the NO I.D. hotline? Are you still there?

> *(He turns to the phone receiver.)*

ANDREW. Yep, still here. I'm not sure HMRC is going to want to hear any of what you've just told me.

TATENDA. Mm.

ANDREW. Are we getting to the part where you deal with changing your name?

TATENDA. No, we're getting to the part where I'm busy hitting puberty and stuff.

ANDREW. Oh, of course, how's that been?

TATENDA. You really wanna know?

ANDREW. Yeah, go on!

(A video plays: it's a compilation of some of **TATENDA**'s *testosterone vlogs.* **TATENDA** *watches along. They're all still up on YouTube for you to enjoy.)*

TATENDA. Puberty is so crazy.

I wish I could tell you I remember what those first six months were really like. I'm so glad I got it on tape. The whole thing is engulfed in a hormonal fog looking back on it now. But it was fun! Every day was exciting. Nobody knew who on earth I was going to be at any given moment, least of all me.

What kind of a guy was I gonna be? So many choices…

I could be an incel, a finance bro, a young and absent father, an emotional abuser, a fuckboy, a softboy, a hardboy? I'm not sure that's one of them?

I did the skater boy thing for a bit, but then people started realising how bad I was at skating, so I had to dilute it with some of this… old-man-who-feeds-pigeons sort of energy…

ANDREW. Mr. Shamiso, you're getting distracted.

TATENDA. Shit, sorry. You're right. Okay.

About seven months into my transition is when I finally felt ready to bite the bullet. Two passports, four countries, what's it gonna take to set my record straight.

> *(**TATENDA** sighs. He doesn't wanna get into it.)*

This is the part where my entire life happens on the phone.

> *(We hear snippets of different phone calls.* **TATENDA** *scrambles around the space, tearing through all of the remaining archive boxes, looking for the papers that are required*

of him, trying to place them in any sort of order that might make sense, passing some of the papers to audience members to hold.)

PHONE VOICES. *You're gonna have to fill out an official deed poll.*

– But you're not a British citizen, and you need someone who's lived in the UK for ten years and owns property to vouch for you on that application anyways, so you can't do that –

Sie müssen zuerst mit den Belgischen Botschaft Anfragen –

– Dear Mrs. Van Wesenbeeck, the Belgian embassy in London is not competent in this matter –

T – H – A – N – D – I – W – E –

– The Zimbabwean Ministry of Home Affairs and Cultural Heritage never acknowledged your existence in the first place, there's no name to change here –

– S – H – A – M – I – S – O

You're going to need to sign an unofficial deed poll in the presence of a solicitor. Then you need to get it apostilled by the Foreign and Commonwealth Office –

–It's now the Foreign, Commonwealth and DEVELOPMENT Office –

then mail us a billion forms and some money and we'll change your name –

– you weren't born in Belgium, so you'll have to go straight to Brussels town hall to change the gender marker –

PHONE VOICES. *The state of California requires a court order –*

– it's just two forms with the GP, but we'll have to give you a new NHS number –

– we can't prove you're vaccinated because you've got one jab on one name and another on your current name.

– Mrs. Shamiso, I'll have to pass this to my supervisor –

　　　*(We hear a blaring airhorn, followed by a 'game over' sound. **TATENDA** wraps himself in papers, falling to the floor. The stage is an absolute wreck.)*

　　　(Corny porno music begins to play. Lights shift to red. Sultry vibes.)

TRAUMA PORN

TATENDA. I bet you're desperate to know about my father. I can see it in your faces, you're gagging to know more about my parents. Right here – you're over here thinking – unffff. I know I have mommy issues, but this guy...?

> *(He cycles through sexy poses among the paperwork on the floor.)*

Now some of you are like ha-ha, oh my god, no, we're not here to make those kinds of assumptions. But like... if you're COMFORTABLE ... this is... a SAFE SPACE ... You really can tell us... how WERE things at HOME?

> *(The lights shift back.* **TATENDA** *chills out.)*

My parents are both very clever, and weird. They're hilarious, but the kind of hilarious where they don't know why what they do is so funny. Like many parents, they had dreams for the kind of person I would become, most of which I think I live up to, they both love me very much, and for better or worse, they are doing their very best.

I'm sure you understand that I'll only ever tell you what they're like on their very best behavior. But if you're so desperate for it, fine. I'll give you a little more.

What you're about to hear is my actual father the way he actually talks sometimes. Keep in mind this is a Belgian man who was not raised anywhere near Buckingham Palace. I cannot for the life of me explain how that is the case, but it is.

> *(A recording of* **TATENDA'S DAD** *answering the same prompt other people in his life answered at the top of the show. He has an oddly British Prince sounding accent. I don't know. He just likes it that way.)*

(**TATENDA** *performs a sock puppet show throughout this recording.*)

TATENDA'S DAD. As a little girl, Thandie was the prettiest, most adorable person I had ever met. I became her daddy, and she instantly became my best buddy.

At the age of two, Thandie could not yet read, but she sure could speak. Even at that age she was my favourite conversation partner. We'd talk about anything and everything. As a young girl, Thandie lived more in books than on the playground. She was rather shy, and often seemed to be in a serious, pensive mood. All that changed at the age of seven, when Thandie first went on stage in a children's theatre group. She was often told by her first director, Ms. Boots, "Thandie, you are **not** the director." And was told not to let her voice tower over the voices of her fellow actresses and actors. That was near impossible with her compelling, beautiful and booming voice.

As a teenager, Thandie was the kind of girl who would be so responsible, dependable, loyal and caring towards her friends that she'd occasionally end up in trouble taking the blame for the mischiefs her friends had dragged her into. At least... that's what she told her parents. She started to dress more soberly, and was never super big on makeup or jewellery, except on stage of course. She was more like an adult than a teenager, carrying the weight of the world on her shoulders. I was told to keep it short, and that's hard to do... what I can say is Tatenda, my son, appears to be more lighthearted and happy than Thandie used to be.

TATENDA. *(Removing the sock puppets from his hands.)* Yeah, yeah. I know the end is sweet. But that's honestly not what I'm here to talk about.

I'm actually too busy! I am finally, for once, *in* control of things in my life which I thought were set in stone. And it feels amazing.

Being a boy is busy work! I am raising my own new masculine pubescent self!

I don't know how familiar anyone in the audience is with transitioning into masculinity, but I've at least found you get taught that you don't get to just be a man. You sort of have to earn manhood.

(**TATENDA** *does a ton of push-ups in this section.*)

It feels like being a man is a lot about giving, and doing. About output.

Protecting.

Providing.

Another word that starts with P.

Penis, I guess?

I feel like a lot of what it takes to be a man is elbow-grease. Brute force. Stature.

But a lot of what it takes to be a **good** man is the kind of shit you learn automatically as a lady.

Listening. Emotional intelligence. Basic consideration.

I think I'm getting the best of both worlds. I get to keep the lessons I learned at the beginning of my life. And I'm on steroids, so I can do a lot of push ups.

(*End of push-up nonsense.*)

Being a man is fucking weird, and most days I think there's more ways to get it wrong than there are to get it right. But I think I have everything I need in me to be a good one. It's not uncomfortable. It sits in me easily.

And there've been times when I've liked being my own parent, through moments my real ones couldn't understand. I started marking my own milestones, like when you have a newborn baby.

TATENDA. Eight months on testosterone, I noticed I had started carrying myself differently.

Nine months in, I got my first little hints of facial hair.

Tatenda's first trip to the barber's.

Tatenda's first voice crack (and certainly not his last).

Tatenda's first time getting a 'sorry, boss' instead of a 'you alright, darling' on the street.

Tatenda's first breakup, and Thandie's last.

I did a lot of Thandie's lasts, too.

Thandie's last work shift, for example, happened right under my nose. I worked at the same cafe from when I was eighteen for four years. Sendero Specialty Coffee – best stuff in south London. You should check them out.

After I came out, I was used to living my cushy life at uni as a man, getting my apron on, and immediately morphing from 'bro' to 'sis'.
"Hi, what can I get ya."
"Flat white."
"Right that'll be two ninety."
"Thanks miss."
Classic.
It felt almost fair. Thandie got me the job. I'm five foot zero. I didn't have my lil peach fuzz there to protect me yet. Checks out.

On Thandie's last shift, I was making a coffee and a long-term customer walked in, saw me, and reacted as if she had seen a ghost. She kept her eyes on me the entire time she was in the shop.

She asked the person at the till, "your colleague over there, what's her name?"
My coworker replied, "*his* name is Tatenda."
"Are you **sure** that's not a girl?"
"I'm sure."

"It's just so crazy... there was a girl who used to work here who looked **just** like him."

And with that, Thandie never worked again.

Thandie's last song was probably the hardest, especially because I don't know when it was. I was trying to book in as much time in the cheapest recording studio I could find to get down as much of my voice as it was as possible just in case my singing voice would turn to pure shit on the other end of my transition. I was scared I would end up like one of those horror stories with the little opera boys who hit puberty and then never sing again. I got as much of it down as time would allow, and then at some point I just couldn't keep up with her anymore.

Tatenda's first song is called "kundera". It's about that first breakup.

> *(He plays the song alone, no additional Tatendas or Thandies accompanying him.)*

LONG FACE, LONG BODY
I'M SHORT AND STOCKY
YOU LIFT ME
YOU LIFT ME

ARMS ROUND MY BODY
HOLD IN ATROPHY
I GIVE YOU AGENCY
I GIVE UP CONTROL OVER ME

YOU LIFT UP
MY SICKLY, TREMBLING LIMBS
PROUDLY

YOU SEE THEIR BEAUTY
YOU MAKE IT EASY

BUT I'VE LOST
SIGHT OF
SO MUCH

OF ME
TO THIS
LIGHTNESS
I WANT TO GET HEAVY
I DREAM
OF THINGS
OUTSIDE
OF THIS –

(He stops playing abruptly.)

The rest of it gets even more emo than that. Imma leave it there.

I know Thandie couldn't have written that song. She didn't know she could just say when she was fed up with something, ask for what she wanted, and then sometimes even get it.

She is still around, of course. I'm still always catching myself doing shit I know I learned from her.

Trans people don't often get a chance to talk about this bit. Where you see your old self in the person you become.
Or hear their voice. Or feel their touch against the nape of your neck.
You don't want to tell people about that bit. You're busy proving that this is who you've been all along, and that you're finally free to be it, and that's often true, but it's not the whole story, and, I've just realized, that we still haven't sorted out my name thing, sorry Andrew.

ANDREW. That's okay.

TATENDA. You know what, you're a real one, buddy.

ANDREW. You're a real one too.

TATENDA. Huh.

ANDREW. Everything okay?

TATENDA. Could you say what you just said again?

ANDREW. Everything okay?

TATENDA. No, before that.

ANDREW. Oh, that you're a real one? You're a real one too?

TATENDA. Yeah.

It's just nice to hear someone on the phone say that I'm real.

> (*A song plays. It is called "old friend".* **TATENDA** *wrote the song four months on testosterone. This recorded voice is higher than his current one, and shakier.* **TATENDA** *sings along a little, but gives the recording a lot of room to breathe.*)

MY VOICE GIVES OUT WHEN I'M SINGING NOW
BUT I'LL STILL PLAY IF YOU WANT ME TO
I'LL NEVER SAY WHAT THIS SONG'S ABOUT
YOU'LL STILL SING IT FROM ROOM TO ROOM
CAUSE YOU LOVE ME, YOU DO
YEAH YOU LOVE ME, YOU DO
CAUSE YOU LOVE ME, YOU DO
YEAH YOU LOVE ME, YOU DO

> (*Both previous and current* **TATENDA** *read a letter to the instrumental of "old friend".*)

TATENDA. *Dear Thandiwe*

I didn't realise until now that I'd need a pen and paper to send you a message.

The lights are on, and I'm home

but you're gone.

I'm not quite alone,

you've gone out for a walk along my bones.

Are you lonely?

I'm not used to you tiptoeing

so quietly.

I feel you rollin in my sheets when I'm asleep

and I can't see that I'm still you and you're still me.

> (**Recorded.** *Singing way higher than current* **TATENDA** *can sing it.*)

ANYWAYS,

> (**Live.** *An octave lower.*)

ANYWAYS,

I'M WRITING JUST TO SAY

THANK YOU FOR GIVING ME

THIS SPACE TO BREATHE

IT WASN'T EASY,

NEITHER FOR YOU NOR ME

YOU ALWAYS WERE SO BEAUTIFUL

BUT I HAD TO THROW OUT YOUR CLOTHES.

THEY DIDN'T FIT

BUT I PROMISE

I WON'T FORGET THE WAY YOU LOOKED IN YOUR PROM
DRESS

PRINCESS,

TAKE CARE,

ONE DAY PERHAPS I'LL MEET YOU

WHEREVER IT IS THAT YOU ARE

I'M ME, FOR NOW

BUT WHO'S NEXT?

WHO'S NEXT?

We're not exactly the same person. I know that. But I wouldn't be a damn thing without her.

Tatenda doesn't have a birth certificate. He was born in the United Kingdom, but he isn't British. He's Bantu. Parts of him come from all over. And you're never going to find him in the phone book.

So. I'll get to it when I get to it.

End of Play

Ingram Content Group UK Ltd.
Milton Keynes UK
UKHW022016200423
420514UK00010B/666